Jesus, My Consolation

A Reflective Devotional for Older Adults

Richard J. Beckmen

Speedwell Press

Other titles by Richard J. Beckmen

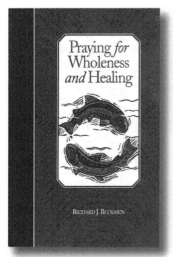  

Praying for Wholeness and Healing
Time for Us: A 30-Day Journey Toward Spiritual Intimacy in Marriage
Prayer: Nurturing Your Relationship with God

For more information, visit www.speedwellpress.com

Jesus, My Consolation: A Reflective Devotional for Older Adults
Richard J. Beckmen

Special thanks to Rev. Rolf & Nancy Olson, Sarah Richter & Karl Olson; Rev. Dr. Harold Taylor; Carol J. Johnson; Mary Ann, Doug & Chaela Manning; Muriel Waage; Joan Olson; Dean Ostlie; James & Sonja Hillestad; John & Bobbie Maakestad.

Jesus, My Consolation

A Reflective Devotional for Older Adults

July, 2019

A gift from my beloved friend, Judy Malone ... with a letter. Perfect timing .... and I melt with joy at the writings within. Help me, Lord, to write my heart on paper waiting for my touch ... to come into the room with a friend needing to be reminded of Your Presence with them — always with us! I was forgetting then this exquisite friend spilled His Love on me. Peace and joy are mine!!

CONTENTS

PREFACE

Writing a book is always a cooperative matter. Memories of conversations, encounters with older adults, who were willing to share their struggles with the life issues of growing older, have contributed greatly to this book.

I wish to thank my mother-in-law for the poems in this volume. Most of them were written in her older years. My gratitude is expressed to Kristina Nockleby, the photographer, who has contributed to the reality of life of older adults through her photographs. She has contributed greatly to the sense of consolation from God through her images.

Paul Nockleby, Publisher at Speedwell Press, is to be thanked for his commitment to produce books that speak to the consolation of healing and grace through God's love which comes to us in our journey through this life.

I commend this book to the many older adults who continue the adventure of living, and desire to grow more deeply in love with God, creation and those who surround their lives.

"Come to me, all you that are weary and are carrying heavy burdens, and I will give you rest. Take my yoke upon you, and learn from me; for I am gentle and humble of heart; and you will find rest for your souls. For my yoke is easy, and my burden is light. Matthew 11:28-30 RSV

INTRODUCTION

Each ongoing segment of our lives has its own questions and mysteries that challenge us to struggle and adapt to a new situation within and around us. The older years are no exception to this. Perhaps the mysteries we face in looking at the present and smaller future ahead are larger than all of the other questions we have faced up to now.

The reflections, poems and Scripture contained in this book are offered in hope they will generate your own insights into your life and the future that remains. It has been my experience that the older we get, the more we can embrace paradox, ambiguity and mystery. What that means is that we begin to give up territory that we thought we had to defend, or prove. This enables us to look more honestly at our struggles, fears, anxieties and hopes. We stand in a broad place now. The broad place and its horizon are not so much on the outside of our lives but on the inside, filled with vast stretches of our memories.

In Luke chapter 24 Jesus comes to walk beside two disciples overcome by Jesus' crucifixion. Their response is probably one of despair at losing a future that seemed to be so promising. Hopes were dashed. They did not recognize Jesus but were affected by his teaching and presence. The disciples invited this seeming stranger to stay with them for supper at the inn. In the breaking of the bread their eyes were opened to recognize Jesus. This story is a powerful reminder that the living Christ journey's with us is in the Word, the Supper and in the loving presence of the consolation of the brethren. He continues to speak into the pain and the joy of our journey.

The reflections in this book are an attempt to write what could be called living psalms. In the psalms of David and the other Biblical writers of psalms, we find the deepest fears, anxieties, joys and hopes of their lives presented to God, hoping for a response of consolation and affirmation. Like the psalms of Scripture, these psalms are an attempt to assist us to write our own psalms that reflect our life story. To find our consolation in life means that we open our hearts and lives to God.

I invite you to begin each chapter by reflectively praying one of the following prayers. Open your mind and heart to the presence of God, the God who has sustained you to this very moment. Take the leap of faith that God will bless you with consolation, wisdom and courage as you open your life to God. At the end of the devotion you are invited to write your own psalm by sharing your questions, concerns, hopes and fears with God. What does the devotion and the Scripture call forth from your life right now?

1) Holy Spirit, Breath of God, You are the promised consolation of Jesus. Whether you come in wind, fire or gentle peace, you empower, encourage, challenge and console my life. I invite your presence into my life in all circumstances, gracious Spirit of God. Come Holy Spirit, into my life, bringing to my remembrance all of the promises of Jesus that can lift my eyes and spirit to the light and love of God.

2) Holy Spirit, you brooded over the chaos and were the instrument of creating order, beauty and promise. Brood over the chaos in my life — restore and renew my life in God and in this creation that I may experience the hope and joy that is promised in redemptive love.

3) O Christ, may your loving presence in my life and in the world always continue to bring consolation to your brothers and sisters. We long for the manifestation of the deep sacrificial love that heals and renews us and the whole creation.

4) O God, give me a fresh understanding and experience of the promise you made so long ago to your people who were caught in captivity. Let this verse ring true for me in my captivity to age and diminishing strength of senses.

But now thus says the Lord, he who created you, O Jacob, he who formed you, O Israel: do not fear, for I have redeemed you; I have called you by name, you are mine. When you pass through the waters, I will be with you; and through the rivers, they shall not overwhelm you; when you walk through the fire you shall not be burned and the flames will not consume you. Isaiah 43:1-3

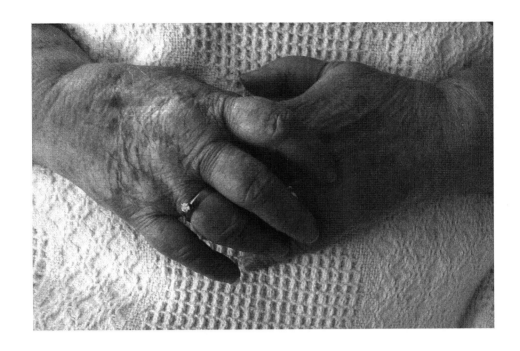

I ALWAYS STAND IN AWE

I always stand in awe of ancient things,
    in both nature and history.
The old white pine with the ancient lightning strike scar,
The broken but recognizable statue of Caesar at Ephesus,
The gnarled hands of the old woman displaying the marks
    of the toil of love.
The pine is too scarred by fire to make good boards,
The statue's fine lines are erased by wind and rain,
The bent hands no longer sew.
But I always stand in awe of ancient things,
    in both nature and history.
Patience,
    Endurance,
        Long-suffering
            have carved a wisdom into these ancient things
    that should be honored and received with awe.
Richard Beckmen

TREASURED GIFTS

Jesus, my consolation,
I hold on to a few treasured gifts from family and friends.
I need them to help me remember that I have been and still
am loved by others.
Some of these gifts I keep for inspiration, some for the good
feelings they engender within me.
I guess those are the reasons I keep so many crosses, icons and
pictures on the walls. I dare not forget or take for granted
the gifts of creation, salvation and the promises you have
given for today and forever.
Remembering through these treasured gifts causes my heart
to be grateful in each new day you give to me.
Help me to remember myself, as well, as being a treasure to
myself and others.
Thank you for the gift of naming me the apple of your eye.

Scripture

*Every generous act of giving, with every perfect gift, is from above,
coming down from the Father of lights, with whom there is no
variation or shadow due to change. James 1:17*

*For this reason I remind you to rekindle the gift of God that is within
you through the laying on of hands. For God did not give us a spirit
of cowardice, but rather a spirit of power and of love and of self-
discipline. II Timothy 1:7-8*

GRANDMOTHER'S CANDLESTICK

I cherish the gift you gave me,
This lovely burnished candlestick.
It lit your way across the sea
Of loneliness, for home nigh sick.
As prairie days stretched on and on
By its light you spun and knit and sought
To make a home, to help each son
Catch dreams of greatness beyond thought.

Sweet grandmother, you were a light,
Serene and clear like crystal day.
Sophisticated, brazen night,
Where lights are mocking, gay
Was not of you. On your heart's altar
A torch was placed. I must not falter.

Agnes Maakestad

REMEMBERING

Jesus, my consolation,
I am not always understood by those around me.
But you are my constant friend.
When I remember some past pain and withdraw into sorrowed
    solitude, others read it as rejection of them.
But you know that when I am caught up in my memories, I
    am not rejecting others.
I am touching my life, my history, which tells me that I have
    lived.
Be in my memories, Holy Spirit, that they may be a joy and
    blessing to me.
Pour love into my heart that I may feel all negative memories
    healed by your grace.
Jesus, make my remembering a time of peace and joy.

Scripture

*This is my commandment, that you should love one another as I
have loved you. I do not call you servants any longer, because the
servant does not know what the master is doing; but I have called
you friends, because I have made known to you everything that I
have heard from my father. John 15: 12, 14-15*

HEAVEN

Jesus, my consolation,
They tell me heaven is my home. Heaven seems like such a
    strange place to me because I have never been there.
I understand this room and its surrounding.
I understand the neighborhood and all the places I have
    visited.
Why don't people understand how important this room is,
    and my neighbors and thousands I don't even know, who
    have touched my life?
I still have something to say about this world.
People could learn from me as I can learn from them.
Heaven can wait for its time.
I still have work to do here, in this place, this room.
Jesus, I am not unmindful of the hope you have given me.
There is a tomorrow in which I will experience all the joy and
    beauty of my eternal home in God's blessed mansion.
But you are here also, and I will live this day in your
    presence.
Jesus, my consolation, help me know the meaning of each day
    that I live.

Scripture

*Do not let your hearts be troubled. Believe in God, believe also in
me. In my Father's house there are many dwelling-places. If it were
not so, would I have told you that I go to prepare a place for you?
And if I go and prepare a place for you, I will come again and will
take you to myself. John 14:1-3*

DOUBT AND FAITH

Jesus, my consolation,
My mind struggles so often with doubt and faith.
Jesus, I know you have lived, died, and are living still.
Come to me in my doubts and touch a spark of faith that I
    may burn brightly with unending hope.
So many times I am like your friend and disciple, Thomas
    — questions, questions and more questions, when there
    should be trust and confidence to believe and to act.
So many times I seek proofs that will lift me beyond the need
    for faith and trust in your Word.
I look for signs and sounds and others' opinions that will
    assure me that you are near.
Teach me, even now, to live by faith in the face of doubt.
Holy Spirit you are the courage of faith. Give me your presence
    that courage may be mine.

Scripture

*Teacher, I brought you my son; he has a spirit that makes him unable
to speak. Bring him to me. Jesus asked, "How long has this been
happening to him?" And he said, "From childhood." The man said,
"If you are able to do anything have pity on us and help us." Jesus
said to him, "If you are able—all things can be done, for the one who
believes." Immediately the father of the child cried out, "I believe,
help my unbelief!" Mark 9:17-25*

TOMORROW

Jesus, my consolation,
I often wonder about tomorrow.
Tomorrow is a time that has yet to arrive.
Is tomorrow really so important?
I have lived so many yesterdays that my days are filled with
the memories of singing, loving, crying, helping, being
angry, and forgiving.
Even today my thoughts are with the memories of the past.
Dare I think of tomorrow?
Yes, I must. Tomorrow will be filled with more life, with you,
gracious Lord, and with those who are near to me, my
consoling One.
I will live toward tomorrow.
Tomorrow belongs to the old as well as to the young.
Our time of worth does not end with yesterday or even
today.
I know tomorrow will be your gift to me.

Scripture

*Jesus said, "So do not worry about tomorrow; for tomorrow will
bring worries of its own. Today's trouble is enough for today."
Matthew 6:34*

*Jesus said, "Do not be afraid, little flock, for it is your Father's good
pleasure to give you the kingdom." Luke12:32*

DEATH

Jesus, my consolation,

Death often seems to come close these days.

So many friends are no longer present to me.

I am glad for the memories of life with these friends — laughter, tears, and, at times, boredom.

Each passing of a friend reminds me of my own appointment with death.

I cling to the consoling passage in Psalm 23, "Yea though I walk through the valley of the shadow of death, I fear no evil, for thou art with me. Thy rod and thy staff they comfort me."

When my hour comes to walk through the valley of that shadow, Jesus, be near to me with your consoling presence.

Be near me just as you have been close to me in all the shadowy places of my life.

Scripture

But if Christ is in you, though the body is dead because of sin, the Spirit is alive because of righteousness. If the Spirit of him who raised Jesus from the dead dwells in you, he who raised Christ from the dead will give life to your mortal bodies also through his Spirit that dwells in you. Romans 8:10-11

IT IS NOT DEATH

If I should die, no morbid pageantry
May pass around my bier, I want no maze
Of lost regret, no poignant threnody
Of muted, mournful grief; no lofty praise.
When I am gone, these gracious gifts be all:
One melody of children's artless song,
One golden daffodil, one candle tall,
To burn serenely pure, steadfast, strong.

And you would bear me to our wind-swept hill,
Close-clasped in your kind arms, no barriers now
To thwart, bewilder, sever us at will.
Winds would chant a requiem, flowers bow
But we, high hearts attuned to ecstasy,
Shall not be grieved; we have eternity.

Agnes Maakestad

SEEING

Jesus, my consolation,
Seeing is such a mixed blessing.
I have seen things in my long life that have brought me joy
    and peace.
I have seen things that made me fearful and anxious.
I have seen things that have been signs of your presence.
I have seen you in the faces of those who love me.
I have seen you in the faces of the poor.
Seeing has helped me understand the work you have called
    me to be about:
Justice for those I see at the margins of life;
Love for those abandoned and misunderstood.
I thank you, Jesus, for opening my eyes to the path that I have
    sought to follow.
I have not always seen what you wanted me to see.
Forgive me for those lost moments.

Scripture

Your word is a lamp to my feet and a light to my path. Psalm 119:105

As they came near the village to which they were going, he walked ahead as if he were going on. But they urged him strongly, saying, "Stay with us, because it is almost evening and the day is now nearly over." So he went in to stay with them. When he was at the table with them, he took bread, blessed and broke it, and gave it to them. Then their eyes were opened and they recognized Jesus and he vanished from their sight. Luke 24:28-31

MY BODY

Jesus, my consolation,
You were a body as I am a body.
You know what I feel and experience.
This body has served me well.
It has made me present to this world and all of its rich experience.
My eyes have looked on happy children running home from school.
My ears have heard the wonderful phrase, "I love you", from my lover.
The intoxicating smell of lilacs in the spring has filled my nostrils.
The taste of cool, fresh water from a bubbling creek has quenched my thirst.
The touch of loving hands has stirred my passion.
The touch of caring hands has eased my pain.
Knowing that you were fully human Jesus, helps me appreciate and delight in being human as well.
Jesus, my consolation, help me always to accept my body and celebrate the gift it has been. I know it is temporary and often carries the pain of change and discomfort.
I look forward to the new heavenly body in the resurrection.

Scripture

So it is with the resurrection of the dead. What is sown is perishable, what is raised is imperishable. It is sown in dishonor, it is raised in glory. It is sown in weakness, it is raised in power. It is sown a physical body, it is raised a spiritual body. If there is a physical body, there is also a spiritual body. I Corinthians 15:42-44

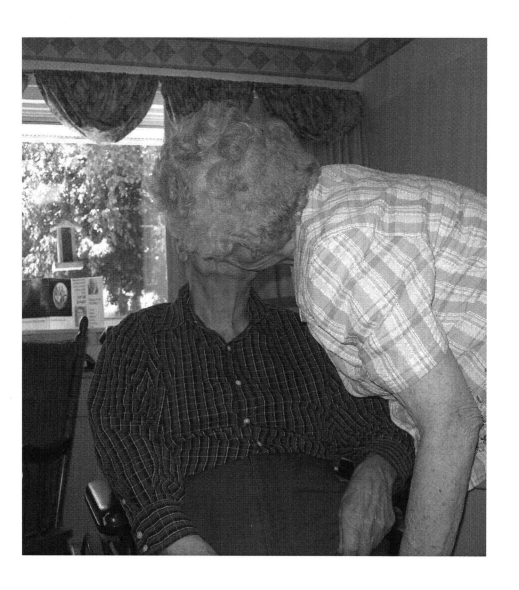

FEELINGS

Jesus, my consolation,
How strange that my feelings have not grown old. The passion
    for life and its experience still move strongly within me.
Joy, anger, fear, sorrow, love, hope — all of these are a part of
    me every day.
So many people do not understand how strong the feelings
    are even though my body moves more slowly and my
    mind wanders so easily, and forgets even the most recent
    event.
Many treat me like a small, recalcitrant child at times, not
    realizing how strong my feelings are, perhaps even
    stronger than their middle-aged boredom and cynicism.
My longings and yearnings are still the same:
    to be loved,
    to be touched,
    to be recognized,
    to matter.
Jesus, my consolation, I yearn for the energy that comes when
    I am conscious of your presence.

Scripture

*So we do not lose heart. Even though our outer nature is wasting
away, our inner nature is being renewed day by day. For this slight
momentary affliction is preparing us for an eternal weight of glory
beyond all measure, because we look not at what can be seen but
what cannot be seen; for what can be seen is temporary, but what
cannot be seen is eternal. II Corinthians 4:16-18*

HUMOR

Jesus, my consolation,
I smile and laugh a lot when I am alone.
I remember so many times of joking, irony and just plain
silliness.
Those times were not contrived, but were actual moments of
real life, appearing as out-of-joint moments to be sure,
I have not lost my sense of humor, but no one seems to tell
many jokes when I am around.
Do they think old age is humorless? I know it isn't. In fact,
there are more things to laugh at within the context of old
age than perhaps at any other time of life.
Holy Spirit, help me maintain my sense of humor.
I have seen both sides of life, and I hope I know when to laugh
and when to cry.
The deepest joy and laughter comes when I recognize that
you are present to my life with grace and freedom.
There is a great deal of humor when you consider that such a
creature as I can carry within me the very Spirit of God.
I continue to desire to be tickled by you, my smiling and
grace-filled consolation.

Scripture

*For everything there is a season, and a time for every matter under
heaven: a time to be born, and a time to die; a time to plant, and a
time to pluck up what is planted; a time to kill, and a time to heal;
a time to break down, and a time to build up; a time to weep, and
a time to laugh; a time to mourn, and a time to dance; a time to
embrace, and a time to refrain from embracing. Ecclesiastes 3:1-5*

CHILDREN

Jesus, my consolation,
Be present to my children and all the other children related
    to me —
Nieces, nephews, grandchildren
and the youngsters from the neighborhood.
They wander and roam about the world.
They remember me and they forget me.
They remember you and they forget you.
They are good and they are bad.
Do not forget them, Jesus, nor forsake them.
Go with them in their work and in their play.
Forgive their sins when they call upon you in repentance.
Lighten their way to your joyful presence.
Jesus, my consolation, be their comfort as well as mine as I
    remember their struggles and their accomplishments.

Scripture

People were bringing little children to Jesus in order that he might touch them; and the disciples spoke sternly to them. But when Jesus saw this, he was indignant and said to them, "Let the little children come to me; do not stop them; for it is to such as these that the kingdom of God belongs. Truly I tell you, whoever does not receive the kingdom of God as a little child will never enter it. And he took them up in his arms, laid his hands on them, and blessed them. Mark 10:13-16

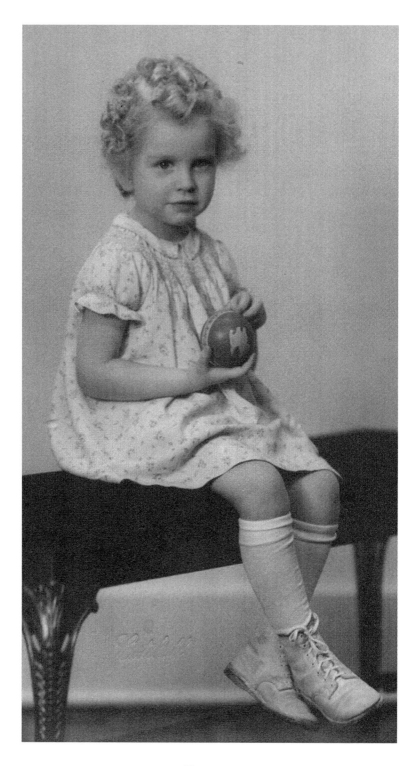

FOR SOLVEIG

One time within my very self you slept;
With every buoyant throb I cherished you;
From bleakest depths, through searing fire, we leapt
Into a radiant day!

I loved your tendril hands, your downy form;
And softly, as the roseate bud uncurled,
A joy, a sense beyond compare was born,
My glad magnificat!

Life flies on magic wings. Today you're three;
Tomorrow grown — a gracious lass,
I'll wrap my love around you . . .May it be
A vesture — vivid, glad!

Agnes Maakestad

FORGOTTEN

Jesus, my consolation,
I am often forgotten.
My family is busy with the business of living.
I pray that they may remember me.
So many friends no longer come, some cannot.
Some have forgotten where I live.
I pray that they may remember me.
I know I am not absent from your memory, Jesus.
Since baptism my life has been hidden with you in God.
There are some who come to visit, remembering me.
I am grateful for these.
Even when I become forgetful of you, Jesus, remember me.
Jesus, my consolation, help me remember those who were
    important in my life.

Scripture

*I keep the Lord always before me; because he is at my right hand, I
shall not be moved. Therefore my heart is glad and my soul rejoices;
my body also rests secure. For you do not give me up to Sheol, or let
your faithful one see the pit. You show me the path of life, in your
presence there is fullness of joy; in your right hand are pleasures
forevermore. Psalm 16:8-11*

INTROSPECTION
(Thoughts when living in a nursing home)

I am alone! The secretive woods
Beckon me to lose myself
In complete oblivion. The green expanse
Shades into a mysterious vista.
Why am I here?

Dear God, please give me a star,
A light to find the one who needs
My solace.
Give the patience I lacked when young and free.
Now I am alone.
The days move on in repetitive
Sameness.

One day the brass-bound doors
Will open to welcome acceptance.
I will leap and dance and fling my arms
Exultantly!
Thankfully!

Agnes Maakestad

JOY

Jesus, my consolation,
I often confuse happiness and joy.
In my mind happiness is the product of the outside environment:
>blue skies,
>a compliment,
>plenty of cash,
>everybody liking me.

Joy, on the other hand, seems to me to flow from the inside out:
>renewal of spirit,
>reconciliation,
>reunion,
>revival.

I associate joy with the Holy Spirit's work in my life.
Joy is one part of the fruit of the Holy Spirit.
Where do I look when a sadness or despair invades my heart
and mind?
I am forever learning again and again to seek the presence of
the Spirit.
It is nice to be happy and to enjoy a pleasant environment.
It is profound joy to live in the Spirit.
Come Holy Spirit, my consolation and deep joy.

Scripture

*Create in me a clean heart, O God, and renew a right spirit within
me. Do not cast me away from your presence; and do not take your
holy spirit from me. Restore to me the joy of your salvation, and
sustain me in a willing spirit. Psalm 51:1-12*

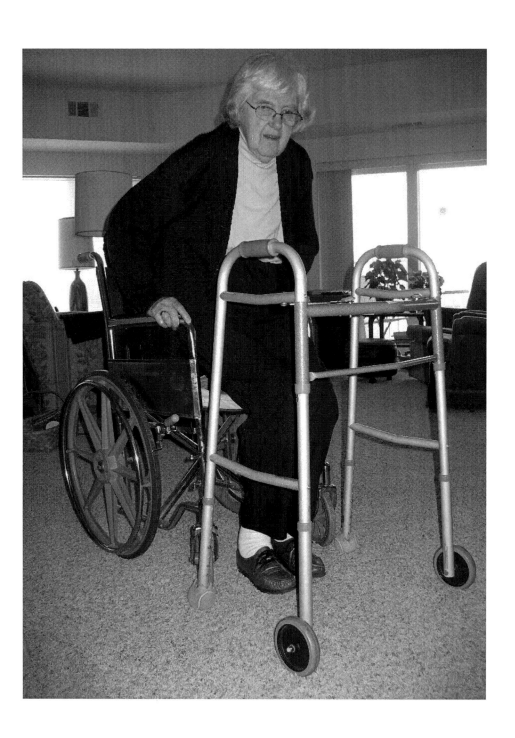

PATIENCE

Jesus, my consolation,
I wonder just how many hours throughout my life I have had
    to wait for something.
Waiting never seems to end. I tire of it, especially at this stage
    of life.
Sometimes, O God, I get agitated that you seem to keep me
    waiting a lot.
But, when I stop and think about it, waiting is your constant
    suggestion.
You do know me so well.
I am always so eager to get going, and get moving.
I, along with many, want to make it happen.
I find it hard to let it happen according to your will.
In your Word, O Lord, I often hear the word "wait!"
I guess that could mean, live the moment I am in and do not
    try to get ahead of you, my Lord.

Scripture

Let your gentleness be known to everyone. The Lord is near. Do not worry about anything, but in everything, by prayer and supplication with thanksgiving let your requests be made known to God. And the peace of God, which surpasses all understanding, will guard your hearts and minds in Christ Jesus. Philippians 4:5-7

I waited patiently for the Lord; he inclined to me and heard my cry. He put a new song in my mouth, a song of praise to our God. Psalm 40:1, 3

Wait for the Lord; be strong, and let your heart take courage; wait for the Lord. Psalm 27:14

KINDNESS

Jesus, my consolation,
I have always hoped that I would not turn into a crabby old
    person.
I guess that if I haven't taken care of all those things that have
    upset me all my life, I will probably be that crabby old
    person.
Is it too late to take care of old business, my Lord?
Holding on to resentments:
    Feelings of failure at certain points in my life;
    Failing to ask for forgiveness or to give it;
    Regretting major decisions that were wrong;
    Failing to respond to persons in desperate need.
I am aware that I have been unkind in so many situations.
I know that your love and grace can work miracles of
    change.
I ask for that miracle to unfold in these later years so that I can
    carry out your teaching in what we call the "golden rule"
    — "Do unto others what you would have others do unto
    you."
Jesus, my consolation, lead me more deeply into your love so
    that my "crabbiness" may be transformed into kindness.
Help me, Lord, to have the strength to give you all my burdens
    that harden my heart.

Scripture

*As God's chosen ones, holy and beloved, clothe yourselves with
compassion, kindness, humility, meekness, and patience. Bear
with one another and, if anyone has a complaint against another,
forgive each other; just as the Lord has forgiven you, so also you
must forgive. Above all, clothe yourselves with love, which binds
everything together in perfect harmony. Colossians 3:12-14*

HOLY COMMUNION

Jesus, my consolation,
What a wonderful gift — a simple meal of bread and wine,
    yet, how complex and mysterious.
There have been so many arguments about the meaning of
    this meal.
Often I try to place myself back to the beginning, to that table
    in the upper room.
How wonderful is the mystery you revealed —
Life-sustaining grace,
    the joy of divine presence.
I know, Jesus, that grace is always a surprise. I suppose that is
    why each taking of the Sacrament is different.
Sometimes, this meal seems so ordinary.
At other times it is so powerful.
Oh Jesus, my consolation, I do yearn for the taste of this grace
    and the aroma of your love.

Scripture

While they were eating, Jesus took a loaf of bread, and after blessing it he broke it, gave it to his disciples and said, "Take, eat, this is my body." Then he took a cup, and after giving thanks he gave it to them, saying "Drink from it, all of you; for this is my blood of the covenant, which is poured out for many for the forgiveness of sins."
Matthew 26:26-28

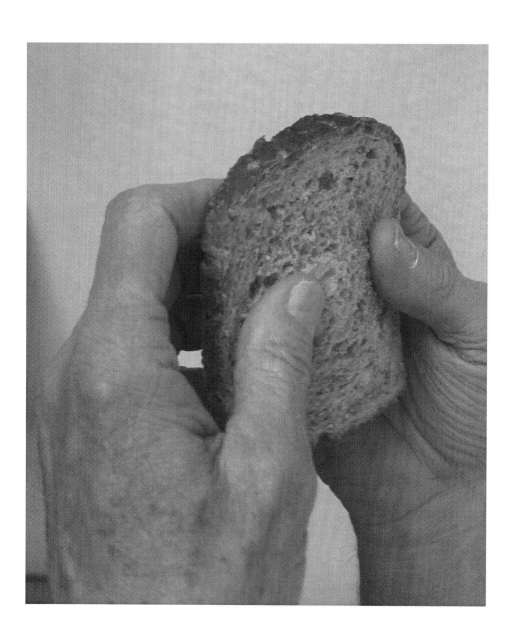

EUCHARISTIC JOY

With such great joy
    I stretch out my hand to receive my Lord.
I strain to match with gladness
    The love I feel in this gift,
    Of bread and wine made more real and life-giving;
Taken in the shadow of that great cross
    Lifted high above;
Calling me to dream a dream
    Of grace upon grace.
Flooding each cell,
    forcing joy into each image that rushes through my mind,
Until there is no room
    for contrition's sorrow or self-inflicted shame.
Only light, as even my shadowed self
    is touched by the delicious taste
    Of Body that is true Bread
    And wine that is Spirit of the Living God.
Such love!
Given and shed,
    For me, for me.

Richard Beckmen

GRANDPARENTS

Jesus, my consolation,
Who would have known how much fun it would be to have
    grandchildren?
Grandchildren are one of the great surprises of God's grace.
I love how easily these little ones put joy into my life.
I relish what they draw from me. They are little muses who
    inspire a creative response
    just by their presence.
They have the capacity to enable us oldsters to act like stand-
    up comedians. They actually laugh at my jokes.
My two-year-old granddaughter was sitting in the back seat
    of the car with her eyes tightly shut. I asked her what she
    was doing. She calmly replied, "I am hiding behind my
    eyes."
Jesus, my consolation, empower me to share a clear testimony
    of faith to my grandchildren.
God, thank you for the generation after generation of our
    children. They help us all see the wit and wisdom of life
    that comes from the honesty and freedom to speak the
    truth they see. Keep our grandchildren from becoming
    cynical and bored as happens to so many of us humans as
    we move through life.

Scripture

*I am grateful to God—whom I worship with a clear conscience; as
my ancestors did—when I remember you constantly in my prayers
night and day. Recalling your tears, I long to see you, so that I may
be filled with joy. I am reminded of your sincere faith, a faith that
lived first in your grandmother Lois and your mother Eunice and
now, I am sure, lives in you. II Timothy 1:3-5*

ON BEING A GRANDMOTHER

Time, how brief!
Time to be a grandmother!
Time to recall the autumn-haired child
Pursuing pussy willows in slushy spring.
The supple girl slaloming giddily down a
    Snow-packed hill.
Time to dream of college, giants who changed
    Your thinking.
Will-o'-the-wisp romantic episodes;
The solemn pledge of marriage;
The solemn parting in death.
All these are my picture album.

But now!
The children, eleven of them:
Tow-haired, red-haired, touch of German,
    Hint of Irish,
Merry-hearted, honest, frank with grandma.
"Grandma, I like you better thin."
"Grandma, I like visiting you."
"Grandma, did you really swim across Glenwood Lake
    And touch the Matterhorn?"
I do not greatly aspire for you.
The plodding days have left their due.
Could I grant these gracious gifts;
Some obligation to a sturdy heritage,
Courage to fulfill your deepest dream,
Protection from bitterness and greed.
Finally,
To think of grandma
With honesty, respect and a special
Uniqueness of Love.

Agnes Maakestad

59

PAIN

Jesus, my consolation,
There are so many kinds of pain.
I have known some of them in varying degrees.
The body pains can have so many effects — distraction, just
plain hurt, or frustration and anger.
The heart has its pains as well — disappointment, broken
relationships, losses of many kinds.
My spirit, as I am reminded by the Apostle Paul, also has its
"groanings" — deep-seated guilt, neglect of time for prayer
and intimacy with God and others who are close and
becoming overwhelmed by the world and its demands.
So often I have resigned myself to some of these pains in order
to get attention or just because of being tired of fighting
the pain.
Bring healing to my pain, gracious Spirit, even as you bring
consolation. Help me not reject that part of myself that is
bringing me pain.
Continue to empower me to love my whole self, my Consoling
One.

Scripture

*Are any among you suffering? They should pray. Are any cheerful?
They should sing songs of praise. Are any among you sick? They
should call for the elders of the church and have them pray over them,
anointing them with oil in the name of the Lord. The prayer of faith
will save the sick, and the Lord will raise them up; and anyone who
has committed sins will be forgiven. Therefore confess your sins to
one another and pray for one another, so that you may be healed. The
prayer of the righteous is powerful and effective. James 5:13-16*

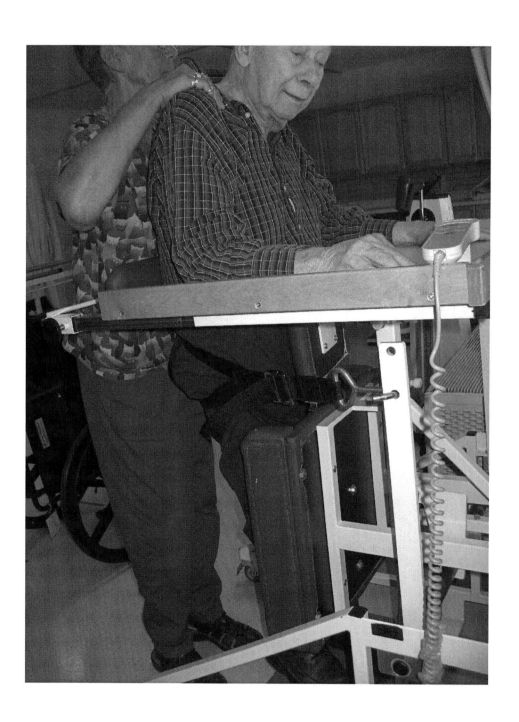

BEING "BOSSED AROUND"

Jesus, my consolation,

Help me remember that I have been set free in God's grace to be me.

Growing older can be difficult at times because so many others, well intentioned usually, want to run my life

I never have liked being "bossed around".

I know a time is coming when others may have to make important decisions about my life because my judgment may be diminished.

But, until then, give me the courage of heart to claim my life and to have the pleasure of risking being free to decide how to live.

Help me also, gracious God, to understand that most of those who work with me — family, doctors, nurses and others — all have a concern for my welfare, and keep the wisdom of my heart working so that I do not reject those who love me.

Continue to strengthen my faith, gracious Lord, so that I do not fail to seek your will above mine.

Scripture

I have been crucified with Christ; and it is no longer I who live, but it is Christ who lives in me. And the life I now live in the flesh, I live by faith in the Son of God, who loved me and gave himself for me. Galatians 2:19-20

REGRETS

Jesus, my consolation,
Regrets! All humans have them.
I have my own little box of regrets, hidden deep in my
    memory.
I take them out of the box once in a while and look at them.
Sometimes they seem to come out of the box by themselves.
    They bring sorrow.
    They bring frustration.
    They bring pain.
    They bring anger, toward myself and toward others.
Jesus, my consolation,
Give me courage through your Spirit to surrender my regrets
    to your invitation to take my burdens.

Scripture

Jesus said, 'Come to me, all you that are weary and are carrying heavy burdens, and I will give you rest. Take my yoke upon you, and learn from me; for I am gentle and humble in heart, and you will find rest for your souls. For my yoke is easy and my burden is light." Matthew 11:28-30

SILENCE

Jesus, my consolation,
I did not realize that there would be so much silence as I
   entered my later years.
Silence seemed both threatening as a younger person and
   often a waste of time.
I am now struggling to capture the joy and gift of silence.
As I wait in silence I am learning to expect the gift of your
   presence.
I am beginning to experience the yearning the psalmist
   recognized within himself and shared it in this verse, "For
   God alone my soul in silence waits."
Silence is the arena in which God engages my soul in
   intimacy.
I wish I had discovered this truth earlier in my life.
But I am glad that there is still time to learn the lessons of love
   from God in the silent waiting.

Scripture

For God alone my soul waits in silence; from him comes my salvation.
He alone is my rock and my salvation. For God alone my soul waits
in silence, for my hope is from him. Psalm 62:1-2, 5

For thus says the Lord God, the Holy One of Israel; in returning
and rest you shall be saved; in quietness and in trust shall be your
strength. Isaiah 30:15

Come, behold the works of the Lord; see what desolations he has
brought upon the earth. He makes wars cease to the end of the earth;
he breaks the bow and shatters the spear; he burns the shields with
fire. Be still and know that I am God! I am exalted among the nations.
Psalm 46:8-10

ON LOSING A CHILD

Jesus, my consolation,
It will never seem right and just that a child should die before
its parents.
How many parents have felt the pain of loss and the numbing
of a promise — watching some future snatched away.
The emptiness lingers and the ache for something to fill the
void is persistent.
This is one more challenge that some face in life — surrendering
again to the mystery of life and death, and life continuing
in the promise of the Creator who is also the author of
resurrection.
Jesus, my consolation, fill my aching void with your comforting
presence.

Scripture

In the Gospel of Luke there is a story that carries great promise
for children who have died quite young.

*Just then there came a man named Jairus, a leader of the synagogue.
He fell at Jesus' feet and begged him to come to his house, for he had
an only daughter, about twelve years old who was dying. While he
was still speaking someone came from the leader's house to say, your
daughter is dead, do not trouble the teacher anymore." When Jesus
heard this, he replied, "Do not fear. Only believe, and she will be
saved." When he came to the house, he did not allow anyone to enter
with him except Peter, John and James and the child's father and
mother. Jesus told the mourners to stop weeping because she was not
dead, only sleeping. They laughed at him. Jesus took the child by the
hand and called out, "Child, get up." Her spirit returned, and she
got up at once. Then he directed them to give her something to eat.
Luke 8:41-42, 49-55*

MY HEART WILL SING AGAIN

Remembering with mute regret the starkness of that day,
Forever held, a mold of clay and crystallized by pain;
Though life and joy may flow and wane, I hold that moment
     high:
In helpless grief I saw you die. One throbbing dream,
One shining brave, translucent gleam, then all was still.
Now silenced motherhood's deep thrill, of rosy curving
     hands;
More tightly closed the iron bands around my frozen heart.
And yet, dear child, though time apart you live in shining
     cloud,
With loveliness with light endowed, where cruel hate and
     greed
Will never quench immortal seed, the innocent, brave song.
You dwell among a purer throng, a fragile golden thread
Is now my link. I, too, can tread upon that vibrant shore.
Some day my bounded heart can pour its ministyrating flow
Upon your head. With spirit's glow, fulfillment of life's quest
Is now attained. At one in God our souls and hearts can rest.

Agnes Maakestad

RECONCILIATION

Jesus, my consolation,
How broken the world seems today.
There is so much distance between people.
Friends and family are so fragile.
Their peace and harmony seem so easily broken by mistrust, jealousy and greed.
Even within myself I feel the distance and separation from so many people.
Who can I trust? Who will care for me? Who will continue to recognize me?
Do these adolescent anxieties ever end?
Jesus, you came among us to make us one and restore harmony through trust and love.
Jesus, I need your love to empower me to forgive all who have hurt me.
Jesus, I need your love to be free of fear and anxiety that separate me from others.
Jesus, teach me to be light in the midst of this world's darkness.
Jesus, enable me to be a peaceful and healing presence to all who are near me.

Scripture

So if anyone is in Christ, there is a new creation; everything old has passed away; see, everything has become new. All this is from God, who reconciled us to himself through Christ, and has given us the ministry of reconciliation. II Corinthians 5:17-18

Jesus said, "You have heard that it was said, you shall love your neighbor and hate your enemy. But I say to you, love your enemies and pray for those who persecute you, so that you may be children of your Father in heaven. Matthew 5:43-45

TEARS

Jesus, my consolation,

I weep tears of sorrow when I think of close ones separated from me now.

I weep tears of anger when I encounter so many who will not understand us old ones. Do we cause them to be afraid of what is coming for them and their aging process?

I weep tears of joy when I am privileged to share in the celebrations, successes and healings of those around me.

Sometimes I weep for no reason at all.

Holy Spirit, I remember that Jesus was no stranger to tears.

He saw them in the eyes of Mary Magdalene when she experienced the joy of forgiveness and freedom, as well as at the garden tomb as she mourned.

He saw them in Peter's repentant sorrow.

He felt tears on his own face as he stood before the tomb of Lazarus.

Perhaps the Garden of Gethsemane was the most powerful tearful scene of weeping in his life.

Holy Spirit, bless my crying.

May my tears be a witness to my compassion, my love, my sense of justice and the pain I feel in genuine grief.

Comfort me in all my crying, Holy Spirit.

Scripture

As a deer longs for flowing streams, so my soul longs for you, O God. My soul thirsts for God, for the living God. When shall I come and behold the face of God? My tears have been my food day and night, while people say to me, "Where is your God?" Psalm 42:1-3

GRACE

Jesus, my consolation,
I wonder why it is so hard to let go of my sense of guilt over
my failures in life.
I know in my mind God forgives. But my heart seems slow
to trust.
I know God loves me.
I know that grace abounds.
Jesus, do I really need this sense of shame? I long to cast it
aside.
Why do I desire in some strange way to reject grace?
Could it be that I pull away from being forgiven because it
means I am indebted to forgive others.
Jesus, my consolation, flood my soul with the gift of the Spirit
again, so that I may rejoice in grace and not hide from its
invitation for me and others.
I do desire your peace within me.

Scripture

*But God, who is rich in mercy, out of the great love with which he
loved us, even when we were dead through our trespasses, made us
alive together with Christ — by grace you have been saved—and
raised us up with him and seated us with him in the heavenly places
in Christ Jesus. Ephesians 2:4-6*

*Therefore, since we are justified by faith, we have peace with God
through our Lord Jesus Christ, through whom we have obtained
access to this grace in which we stand; and we boast in our hope of
sharing the glory of God. Romans 5:1-2*

IMAGINATION

Jesus, my consolation,
What a gift!
I can hardly measure the worth of my imagination.
So often, when things are falling apart, I tend to imagine the
worst possible outcome. This is one of my traits I am trying
to transform.
Lord, I really do want to imagine more of the best possible
outcome. I don't mean trying to create a fantasy. With the
guidance of the Holy Spirit I want to create a vision of
what could happen in following your path.
Phrases like "What if . . . ."
"Maybe I can . . . ."
"What is the best that could happen?"
"What is the hope here . . . .?"
I am thankful for these phrases which are a call to create.
I am thankful for the Holy Spirit, the Spirit of creativity and
"possibility thinking."
I am thankful for the images and visions the Holy Spirit brings
to my life for the future that still lies ahead of me.
How dull and unexciting life would be without imagination
for the Spirit to inspire.
I take delight in your plans for me, Jesus, my consolation.

Scripture

*I will pour out my Spirit on all flesh; your sons and your daughters
shall prophesy, your old men shall dream dreams, and your young
men shall see visions. Joel 2:28*

*O God, you are my God; I seek you, my soul thirsts for you, as in
a dry land where there is no water. Because your steadfast love is
better than life, my lips will praise you. My soul is satisfied as with
a rich feast, and my mouth praises you with joyful lips when I think
of you on my bed and meditate on you in the watches of the night;
for you have been my help, and in the shadow of your wings I sing
for joy. Psalm 63:1, 3-7*

LOVE

Jesus, my consolation,

My life is fed by the memories of loving and being loved.

Thank you for bringing so many people into my life who could share the depth of your love with me.

I remember my fourth grade teacher. She cared so much for me to succeed. Her love was such an encouragement to dream and study for a bright future.

I am so thankful for the love of parents who let me be and become me.

You gifted me with such a loving and caring spouse who released in me the courage to love and be loved.

So many friends have been in my life as a supporting community of love.

It took me quite a while in my life to understand that love is the soil in which faith and hope can become fully rooted, and emerge to provide a rich and meaningful life.

Of course, love is not only to be received, but to be given as well.

The face of the one I love would shine when I said, "I love you."

A visit to a sick friend, a gift to one with needs, a sharing of time and encouragement are gifts I have been empowered to give because of your love-gift to me, gracious Lord.

And now I look to your consoling love to follow me all the days of my life.

Scripture

I pray that, according to the riches of his glory, he may grant that you may be strengthened in your inner being with power through his Spirit, and that that Christ may dwell in your hearts through faith, as you are being rooted and grounded in love. Ephesians 3:16-17

Love is patient; love is kind; love is not envious or boastful or arrogant or rude. It does not insist on its own way; it is not irritable or resentful; it does not rejoice in wrongdoing, but rejoices in the truth. It bears all things, believes all things, hopes all things, endures all things. I Corinthians 13:4-7

BAPTISM

Jesus, my consolation,

John the Baptist said that Jesus would baptize with fire and the Spirit.

Could that have happened to me-- fire and Spirit?

My folks said it was a quiet time. I slept. The pastor prayed. The people watched. My parents worried that I would cry.

Where was the Spirit? Where was the fire?

Could it be that baptism is now and forever, a day by day burning and learning, dying and rising? Could I be living in my baptism, always living in the stream of God's grace?

Was that quiet baptism the beginning of this burning and breathing me?

Was it that quiet beginning of water and Word that has brought me into this believing, doubting, joyful struggle that is my life in God?

Come Spirit! Come fire! Breathe and burn in me.

I am a child of God!

Scripture

Do you not know that all of us who have been baptized into Christ Jesus were baptized into his death? Therefore we have been buried with him by baptism into death, so that, just as Christ was raised from the dead by the glory of the Father, so we too might walk in newness of life. Romans 6:3-4

HOPE

Jesus, my consolation,

Is there a way to enable hope to grow brighter as I grow older?

I am constantly tempted to look at what I am losing as I live out my life in these later stages.

What I want to remember is how much love and grace I have received from you and from others that have given me a hope to hold on to as I look ahead.

My experience of ongoing forgiveness and divine care has formed a solid base for believing in the bright future with God tomorrow and the forever that lies beyond death.

O God, my consolation, surround me with your protection so that the evil one would not steal the vision of my future with you from my mind and heart.

Scripture

By awesome deeds you answer us with deliverance, O God of our salvation: you are the hope of the ends of the earth and of the farthest seas. Psalm 65:5

Let us hold fast to the confession of our hope without wavering, for he who has promised is faithful. Hebrews 10:23

GRATITUDE

Jesus, my consolation,

What is the key that unlocks my heart to be grateful? I live through so many days unconscious of the grace that is flowing into my life. I need to be more diligent in opening my eyes to your gifts and my heart to your love.

Lord, you delight me with so many surprises. When I am awake to your goodness and kindness, I am truly amazed at your love for me.

It is in those moments that thanksgiving begins to emerge as a feeling, as a song of praise, as a shout of delight.

Knowing your grace, loving Lord, is the source of gratitude that makes life so rich and full.

My soul fills with joy when I lay aside bitterness and self-preoccupation and allow the thought of your promise to be with me and in me forever to dominate my mood and expectations.

I thank you, my Consoling One, with all my heart and strength for the way in which you have called me, sustained me and led me into the delights of your presence and promise.

Scripture

O give thanks to the Lord, for he is good, for his steadfast love endures forever. Psalm 136:1

Rejoice in the Lord always; again I will say, rejoice. Let your gentleness be known to everyone. The Lord is near. Do not worry about anything, but in everything by prayer and supplication with thanksgiving let your requests be made known to God. And the peace of God, which surpasses all understanding, will guard your hearts and mind in Christ Jesus. Philippians 4:4-7

GROWING OLD IN OUR TIME

There is a deep sadness in the eyes of the old in our time. Children and grandchildren no longer come home. Home is no longer there. Like displaced persons in a silent war the old no longer live at home.

They are in the trailer park, a silver bullet, Air Stream on the move, nervously trying to find a history in the ruins of a forgotten America.

They are in town houses, temporary villages without myth or history, neat as a botanical garden, empty of memories.

They are in nursing homes, slightly veneered hospitals, where children feel unwashed guilt, and grandchildren may not run or shout.

There is a deep sadness in the eyes of the old in our time. This is the sadness akin to the fear the old stories will not be told — the ancient scars of swing ropes on the oak tree, the nicks and scratches on the kitchen cabinets and stair banisters.

These held the clues to our story-filled history, etched memories to bring recall of a shared family life. Each scar sparked the telling of the stories of tears, joys, love and events of life lived together. If no one lives at home who will remember?

There is a deep sadness in the eyes of the old in our time.

It is not the uncertain future that kindles the sadness, although the future could do that. It is what will happen to the past that brings wrinkles of anxiety and fear.

The old rejoice in the good times of now for the young. They hope for an even a better time yet to come for the young.

But they also know the power of the legend. They remember the strength of the home, the power of the story created in that well-worn sanctuary. They mourn the passing of the tribe, the village, the house that was a home, the place that was the treasure store of the clues to the story of who we were, and are, and will be.

There is a deep sadness in the eyes of the old in our time.

Richard Beckmen

POSTSCRIPT
Agnes: Poet and Mother

The autumn afternoon when we buried Agnes was spectacular. Indian summer had arrived. A silver harvest moon hung in the sky. The air had a golden haze; autumn leaves — rust-colored oaks, orange-yellow elms, scarlet maples — were scattered among the grave stones.

My mother was no ordinary woman: she was a poet and a musician, a pianist and organist. Her temperament was volatile like her red brown hair. Autumn colors were hers. A bouquet of fall-colored chrysanthemums and a vine of bittersweet were on her casket. Bittersweet was my mother's insignia.

Her creative energies were renewed in nature — swimming Lake Minnewaska, hiking the hills of Glenwood, exploring the woods around Rochester. On a pleasant Saturday she'd say, "Come on kids. Find your shoes. Let's go to the woods." And we'd take buckets and baskets and drive to outlying farms where we would tramp and plunder the woods of nuts and berries, and, sometimes, bittersweet vines. It didn't seem to bother her that we were trespassing on private property. For Mother, the entire out-of-doors was public domain. We'd pile into the '34 Ford and return home with nature's bounty. Other kids' mothers would offer embroidered items for the Ladies Fall Bazaar, but my mother would bring glasses of wild-berry jellies and bunches of bittersweet.

On the first day of fall 1986, Mother had a heart attack. She was hospitalized for three weeks before a final attack. I was thankful for that time of grateful closure. I brought her colorful leaves, and my brother delivered the last rose from the garden and a branch of bittersweet. At the cemetery my pastor-spouse spoke the words of committal and we and our children sang a favorite hymn: "Now thank we all our God...., who from our Mother's arms hast blest us on our way, with countless gifts of love..."

Then we all went to eat by the lake. The moon had become

golden and shimmered across the water. It was a beautiful ending to a bittersweet day.

On the first anniversary of her death, I mourned my mother's absence.

The second year, I was still sad, but at the grocer, I saw bittersweet for sale. When I brought it home, Dick exclaimed, "Yes! In remembrance of your mother."

The third year, Bobbie called, "There will be a full moon on the anniversary of your mother's death, and it's been weeks since we have seen you. Let's get together for a picnic. We'll meet half-way at the regional park at Cleary Lake near Shakopee. We'll bring the famous wieners from our market."

"And I'll get a chocolate cake from the bakery."

We met on another golden Indian-summer day. The trees along the road were ablaze with color — reds and golds. We arrived about the same time. Other families were enjoying the park, and the air was filled with the chatter of children. In addition we heard the insistent honking of geese. There were so many of them, they looked like a bridge across the water. Could we have walked on their backs across the lake? We roasted the wieners, ate potato salad and cake, and finished the coffee. We shared our pictures from our summer jaunts and agreed it was good to be together.

We packed up and decided to explore a bit. I said I wanted to look for dried weeds for a fall bouquet. Bobbie pointed out branches at the base of a tree that would be lovely, and when I went over there, I cried out, "Oh, look! There's bittersweet."

Dick exclaimed, "Your mother's come to the party!" By now the full moon was high in the eastern sky, fingers of clouds brushing across her face. A final hug, and we were on our way. All the way home, the moon was smiling. It was a perfect reunion with an unexpected surprise.

Agnes, thank you for the memories and for your gifts to me and to the world.

Solveig Beckmen, daughter

POSTSCRIPT
Richard: Writer, Mystic and Father

In the early centuries of the church, there was a group of men and women who moved to the wilderness — the desert — where they lived simply. Their purpose was to let go of distractions so they might hear God and experience God's presence. Pilgrims would come out to the desert to spend time with these desert fathers and mothers to grow in their faith and learn to hear God as well.

Richard, in a way, is a contemporary desert father. Richard, or Dick as he is more widely known, is one who has helped people hear God's voice and experience God's gracious presence in their daily lives in the midst of the world.

I have seen him do this from the perspective of daughter. I did not always know he was a contemporary desert father — he was just my father. But, as I have grown, I have come to realize he has had a great impact on many lives of faith. And he has done this because he has let himself be used by God. He is a contemporary contemplative who spends time in prayer, for the purpose of sharing his knowledge and love of God with others.

My father goes to the desert often — sometimes alone, often with family in tow — to renew and hear the voice of God. I remember camping trips, canoeing in the Boundary Waters of Minnesota, climbing mountains, setting up a big blue tent in the wind. In the desert places, I learned from my father, the spirit is renewed and the connection to God is made deeper and more real. I learned to hear the voice of God and see his presence all around.

My father prays. He prays for me each day — twice a day. This is a source of strength. My father prays for many. I know that he gives strength to many. He has taught many to deepen their prayer life. He has taught many to deepen their connection to our gracious and loving God. He has taught me that the heart of discipleship is prayer. Prayer is the source of knowing God personally. It is the daily means to tell God I love him back. This is foundational for everything I do — with my own family, with my parish, with my life.

My mother told me a powerful story when I was writing my senior paper for the seminary. She told me that when my father was writing this same paper, he wrote that he loved Jesus. Dick loves Jesus. His love for his Lord is the foundation of all he does. As he preaches, as he teaches, as he parents, he does all this out of his love for Jesus. As he writes, he opens the door for others to discover that they, too, love Jesus.

He also knows that Jesus loves him. My father has a practice of asking God for a daily question — a question for him to live and to ponder. When he was hospitalized in preparation for heart surgery, Dick asked God for the question. It came. "Do you know how much I love you?" Dick knows he is loved by God. As he preaches, as he teaches, as he parents, he does all this so that others know that God loves them. As he writes, he opens the door for others to discover that they, too, are loved by God.

This desert father who is my father has spent his life as a servant connecting people to the living God, connecting people to our savior, Jesus, helping people know they are loved by a God who knows them by name. I love you, Dad!

Siri Beckmen, daughter

Jesus, My Consolation
A Reflective Devotional for Older Adults
Richard J. Beckmen

This volume presents "living psalms" from Richard Beckmen's life experience, and is intended to assist older adults in opening their hearts and lives to God. Like the psalms of the Bible, these reflections speak prayerfully to God about the deepest sorrows, joys, fears, and hopes of older adults who have been promised to receive consolation and affirmation from God. This book is an attempt to encourage older readers in writing their own psalms reflecting their own circumstances, needs, and life story. Indeed, God comes to us in all kinds of places and times, such as the extremely dark and desolate time after Jesus' crucifixion, recorded in Luke 24, as pictured on the front cover of this book. The Emmaus Road story is a reminder that Christ journeys with us everywhere we go, whether we remember or recognize Him or not, and continues to reveal Himself to us in the Word, in the Supper, and in the consolation of the brethren.

*Pastor Richard J. Beckmen has focused his ministry on nurturing deepening relationships with God through personal prayer disciplines. Author of three previous books (*Prayer: Nurturing Your Relationship with God; Praying for Wholeness and Healing; *and* Time for Us, *a devotional for couples) Pastor Beckmen lives with his wife, Solveig, in Northfield, Minnesota in a community of older adults.*

ISBN 978-0-9822544-3-1

Speedwell Press
Publishing for your pilgrimage

PO Box 131327
Roseville, MN 55113 • USA
www.speedwellpress.com